# Black Beans and Lamb, Poached Eggs and Ham

to Sister Editha, my second-grade teacher in Richfield, Minnesota
—B.P.C.

to my dad, who showed me that knowing beans about something
doesn't mean you're dead meat
—M.G.

Meat and Beans:
The name of a food
group that includes
meat, poultry, fish,
dry beans and peas,
eggs, nuts, and seeds

# Black Beans and Lamb, Poached Eggs and Ham

## What Is in the **Meat and Beans** Group?

by Brian P. Cleary

illustrations by Martin Goneau

consultant Jennifer K. Nelson, Master of Science,
Registered Dietitian, Licensed Dietitian

Ⅶ Millbrook Press • Minneapolis

Meat and poultry, fish and beans, eggs and nuts belong

all in just one food group
that can help us to be strong.

These foods contain B vitamins, and protein, zinc, and iron

that help with muscle growth and keep our nervous systems firin'!

How much of these foods
should we be eating every day?

A 3-to-5-ounce daily dose
is what the doctors say.

That might be a scrambled egg
plus half a chicken breast.

A quarter cup of pinto beans would help you get the rest.

Meats all come from animals,
so if you were to browse

inside the butcher's shop, you'd see the meaty parts of cows,

Poultry comes from certain birds.

It's meat that they produce.

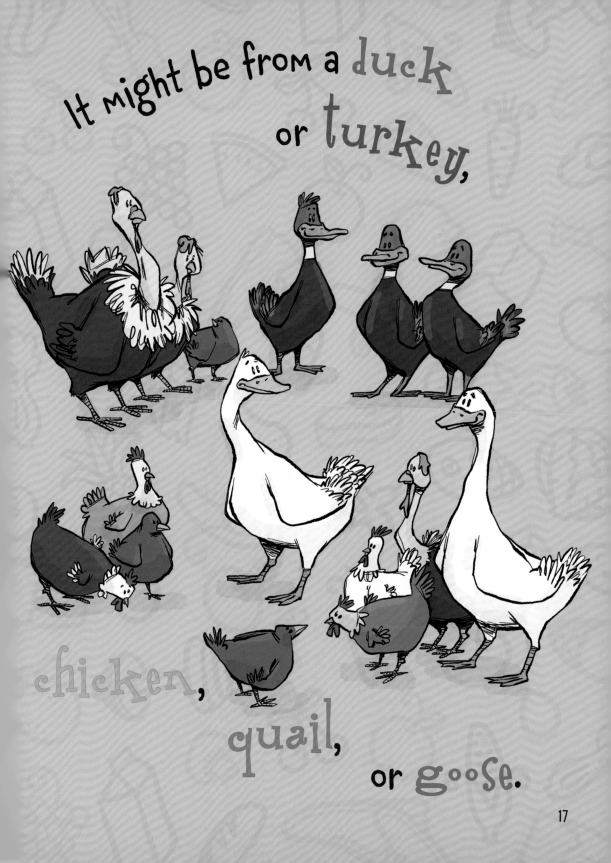

It might be from a duck or turkey,

chicken, quail, or goose.

What else can you have to eat the next time you grill out?

Try tuna, snapper, mackerel fish, some salmon, cod, or trout.

19

Experts say that most of us don't eat enough fresh fish,

They also say that choosing meat and poultry low in fat

will help us to be healthier,

so try to do just that!

Nuts are in this food group
with dry beans,
seeds, and peas.

A nutrient—magnesium— is found in all of these.

It helps our bodies build strong bones. It's also good for muscles.

It benefits our nerves and hearts.

It's a nutrient that hustles!

Nothing "nuts" or "fishy" here—
just think "beef"-fore you bite,

and the choices
that you make each day
can be "eggs"-actly right!

# So what is in the meat and beans group? Do you know?

You should eat 3 to 5 ounces of foods in the meat and beans group every day. The exact amount depends on your age and how much exercise you get. To figure out the right amount for you, visit www.mypyramid.gov and click on MyPyramid Plan.

1 egg equals 1 ounce

1 small soy burger, black bean burger, or ground meat burger equals 2 ounces

1 tablespoon of peanut butter equals 1 ounce

1/2 can of tuna equals 1.5 to 2 ounces

1/4 cup of cooked beans or lentils equals 1 ounce

1 small chicken breast half equals 3 ounces

Find activities, games, and more at
www.brianpcleary.com

This book provides general dietary information for children ages 5–9 in accordance with the MyPyramid guidelines created by the United States Department of Agriculture (USDA). The information in this book is not intended as medical advice. Anyone with food allergies or sensitivities should follow the advice of a physician or other medical professional.

## ABOUT THE AUTHOR, ILLUSTRATOR & CONSULTANT

**BRIAN P. CLEARY** is the author of the Words Are CATegorical®, Math Is CATegorical®, Adventures in Memory™, Sounds Like Reading®, and Food Is CATegorical™ series, as well as several picture books and poetry books. He lives in Cleveland, Ohio.

**MARTIN GONEAU** is the illustrator of the Food Is CATegorical™ series. He lives in Trois-Rivières, Québec.

**JENNIFER K. NELSON** is Director of Clinical Dietetics and Associate Professor in Nutrition at Mayo Clinic in Rochester, Minnesota. She is also a Specialty Medical Editor for nutrition and healthy eating content for MayoClinic.com.

Millbrook Press
A division of Lerner Publishing Group, Inc.
241 First Avenue North
Minneapolis, MN 55401 U.S.A.

Website address: www.lernerbooks.com

Library of Congress Cataloging-in-Publication Data

Cleary, Brian P., 1959–
   Black beans and lamb, poached eggs and ham : what is in the meat and beans group? / by Brian P. Cleary ; illustrated by Martin Goneau ; consultant, Jennifer K. Nelson.
      p.   cm. — (Food Is CATegorical)
   ISBN: 978-1-58013-591-7 (lib. bdg. : alk. paper)
   1. Food of animal origin—Juvenile literature. 2. Beans—Juvenile literature. I. Goneau, Martin. II. Nelson, Jennifer K. III. Title.
   TX558.B4C54 2011
   641.3'06—dc22                                                          2009049572

Manufactured in the United States of America
1 – PC – 7/15/10